December
Decorations

READY-TO-READ
HANDBOOK

December Decorations

A Holiday
How-to Book

by Peggy Parish

Illustrated by Barbara Wolff

Macmillan Publishing Co., Inc.
New York
Collier Macmillan Publishers
London

Macmillan Publishing Co., Inc.
866 Third Avenue, New York, N. Y. 10022
Collier Macmillan Canada, Ltd.
Printed in the United States of America
10 9 8 7 6 5 4 3 2 1

Library of Congress Cataloging in Publication Data
Parish, Peggy.
December decorations.
(A ready-to-read handbook)
1. Holiday decorations—Juvenile literature.
[1. Holiday decorations. 2. Handicraft] I. Wolff,
Barbara. II. Title.
TT900.H6P37   745.59'41   75—14285
ISBN 0—02—769920—X

For Paul Kahn, with love

Contents

December
Decorations

Some Things to Remember

1. Read the whole project before you begin.

2. Have the things you need to work with before you start.

3. Use poster paints, except for gold.

4. Use clean paint brushes.

5. Use a good all-purpose glue.

6. Work on old newspaper.

7. Put things away
   when you finish
   your work.

8. Try out your
   own ideas!

How to Make Salt Clay

1. Put some flour and salt in a bowl. Add water.

2. Mix well.
   If the clay is sticky,
   add a little flour.
   If it is too dry,
   add a little water.

   Salt clay is good
   for making small things.
   But it is not good for big things.
   It takes too long to dry.

Pipe Cleaner Candy Cane

1. Paint a pipe cleaner red.
   Let the paint dry.

2. Twist the red
   and a white pipe cleaner
   around each other.

3. Bend them into a cane shape.

Paper Chains

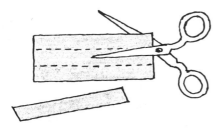

1. Cut colored art paper into strips.

2. Bring the ends of a strip together to make a ring. Staple or glue them in place.

3. Slip another strip through the ring.

Bring the ends of that strip together and staple or glue them in place.

4. Add rings until your chain is as long as you want it.

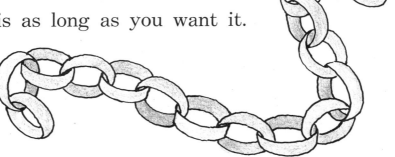

Paper Ring Tree

1. Make 21 paper rings (step 2 at left). Tape or staple them together as shown.

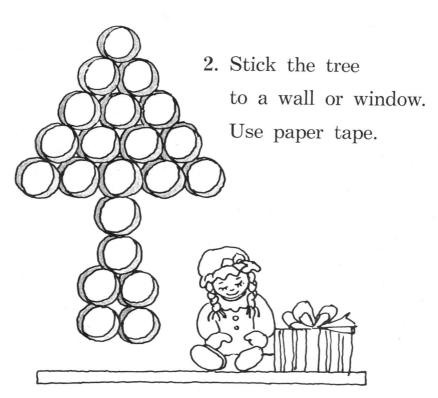

2. Stick the tree to a wall or window. Use paper tape.

Jumping Jack

1. Cut colored art paper in strips. Make one big and one small paper ring (see page 14).

2. Fold two long and two short paper strips as shown.

3. Fold another strip to make a hat.

4. Tape or staple the parts together.

5. Punch a hole through the top of the hat. Put a string through it. Tie the string to make a loop.

Paper Tree Ball

1. Cut three strips from
   colored paper.
   Lay them as shown.
   Staple or glue
   them in place.

2. Bring the ends together
   to make a ball.
   Staple or glue
   the ends in place.

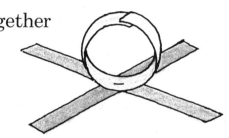

3. Tie a string around a strip
   to make a loop for hanging.

Pasta Wreath

1. Dye some raw pasta
   in food coloring.
   Let it dry on paper.

2. Cut the center
   out of a paper plate.

3. Punch a hole
   in the plate rim.
   Put a string through the hole.
   Tie the string to make a loop.

4. Mix flour and water
to make a sticky paste.
Cover one side of the plate rim
with paste.

5. Cover the paste with
colored pasta. Let it dry.

6. Glue on a ribbon bow.

Yarn Roundabouts

1. Cut a pipe cleaner in half. Twist the pieces together.

2. Tie a piece of yarn to the center. Wrap yarn around the center to cover it.

3. Then wrap yarn over, around, and under each pipe cleaner.

 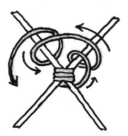 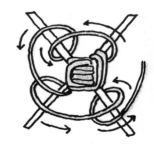

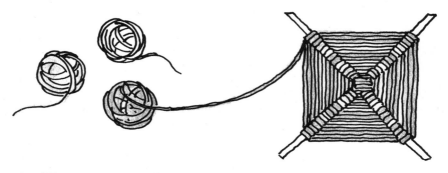

4. To use another color,
   tie the ends of the yarn together.
   Wind until the pipe cleaners
   are almost covered.

5. Tie the end of the yarn
   to one of the pipe cleaners.
   Then tie again
   to make a loop.

Bell

1. Put a string
   through a small jingle bell.

2. Make a small hole
   in the top of a paper cup.
   Put the ends
   of the string
   through the hole.
   Tie the ends
   to make a loop.

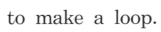

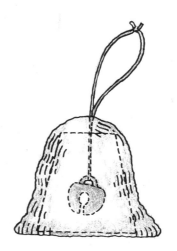

3. Cover the cup
   with salt clay
   (see page 12).
   Shape as shown.
   Keep the loop free.

4. Paint the bell.
   Let it dry for
   a day or two.

Holly Wreath

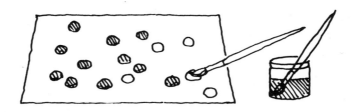

1. Make some small salt clay balls
(see page 12).
Paint them red for holly berries.

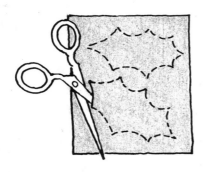

2. Cut out a lot of
holly-shaped leaves
from green paper.

3. Cut the center
out of a paper plate.

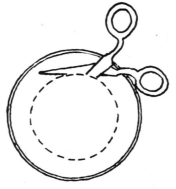

4. Punch a hole
   in the plate rim.
   Put a piece of string
   through the hole.
   Tie the string
   to make a loop.

5. Glue paper holly leaves
   and salt clay berries
   over the plate rim.

6. Glue or staple on
   a ribbon bow.

Candle with Holly Holder

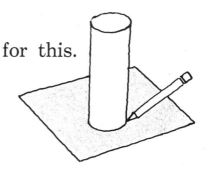

1. Use a cardboard tube for this.
   Draw a circle
   around one end
   on colored paper.

2. Draw a larger circle outside the first.
   Cut as shown by the dotted lines
   below to make tabs.

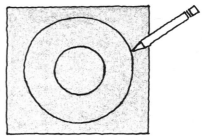

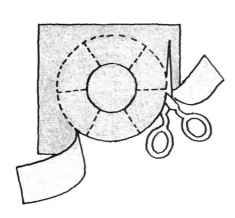

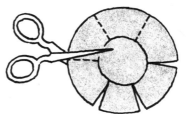

3. Bend the tabs down.
   Glue them to the tube.

4. Cut a wide strip
   of paper
   to cover the tube.
   Glue it in place.

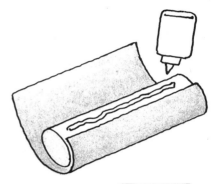

5. Cut a piece of yellow paper
   as shown for the flame.
   Cut a small slit
   in the candle top.
   Slip the flame in place.

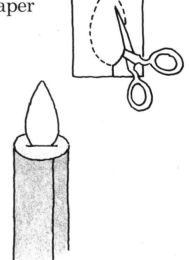

...MORE

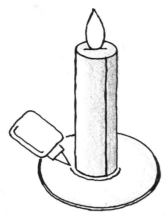

6. Cut a larger circle
from cardboard.
Glue the candle to it.

7. Glue paper holly leaves
and red salt clay berries
(see page 24)
around the candle.

Gold Branches

1. Get some evergreen branches.
   Take off the lower leaves
   or needles.

2. Wipe the other
   leaves or needles
   with a damp sponge.
   Let them dry.
   Then paint them gold.

3. Put the bare ends
   of the branches in water.

29

Holiday Branches

1. Get some branches
   with small twigs on them.

2. Paint part of a branch
   with liquid starch.

3. Shake glitter
   or powdered detergent
   over the wet starch.

4. Do the rest the same way.
   Let the branches dry.

5. Do not put
   the branches
   in water.

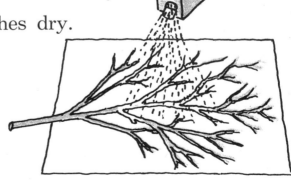

30

Gumdrop Branches

1. Get some branches
   with thorns on them.

2. Wash the branches
   and let them dry.

3. Stick a small gumdrop
   on each thorn.
   Mash the gumdrops down.

4. Do not put
   the branches
   in water.

Eggshell Pictures

1. Dye some eggshells
   with food coloring.
   Let them dry.
   Break them
   into small pieces.

2. Punch a hole in the top
   of a piece of cardboard.
   Put a string
   through the hole.
   Tie the string
   to make a loop.

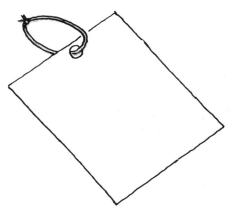

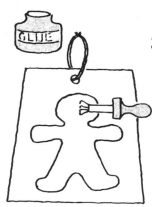

3. Draw a picture
on the cardboard.
Put glue on the picture.
"Paint" it with eggshells.

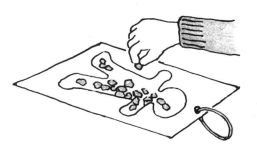

Eggshell Trims

1. Color some eggshell halves
   with paint or food coloring.
   Let them dry.

2. Trim the shells by gluing
   on stars, pictures, glitter,
   or anything you like.

3. Glue a loop of string
   to the top of the shell.
   Let the glue dry.

Stocking

1. Draw a pattern for
   a stocking on paper.
   Cut it out.

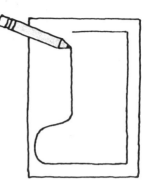

2. Pin the pattern
   to two pieces of cloth.
   Cut around the pattern.

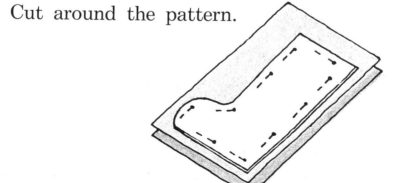

...MORE

3. Trim the stocking shapes as you like.

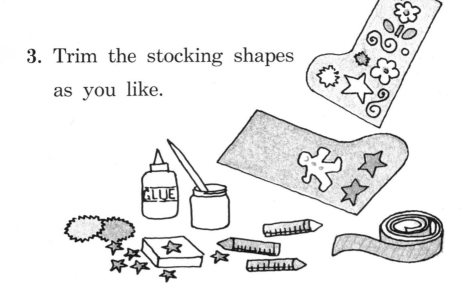

4. Cut some pieces of string to make a handle. Glue the strings to one stocking shape where shown. Put more glue on top.

5. Put glue around the edge
of the stocking as shown.
Leave top open.
Lay the second shape on top.
Press them together.

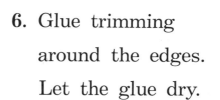

6. Glue trimming
around the edges.
Let the glue dry.

37

Snowflake

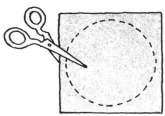

1. Cut a circle from paper.
Fold it in half.
Then fold it in half again.

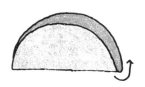

2. Cut out shapes
along the folds.
Unfold.

3. Punch a hole
in the top
of the snowflake.
Put a string through it.
Tie the string
to make a loop.

Fluff Ball

1. Use six snowflakes (see page at left)
   or six paper doilies.
   Fold each in half.
   Then fold them
   in half again
   and once again.
   Punch a hole in each.

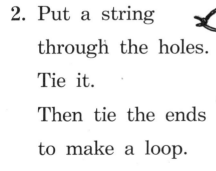

2. Put a string
   through the holes.
   Tie it.
   Then tie the ends
   to make a loop.

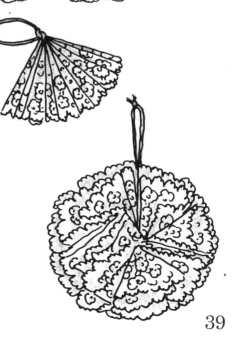

3. Fluff it out
   to make a ball.

Christmas Tree

1. Fold a piece of brown paper
   or newspaper in half.
   Start at the fold.
   Draw a half tree.
   Cut it out.
   This is your pattern.

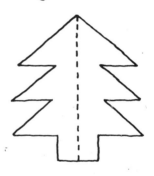

2. With the pattern,
   draw two trees on cardboard.
   Draw four trees
   on green paper.
   Cut out all the trees.

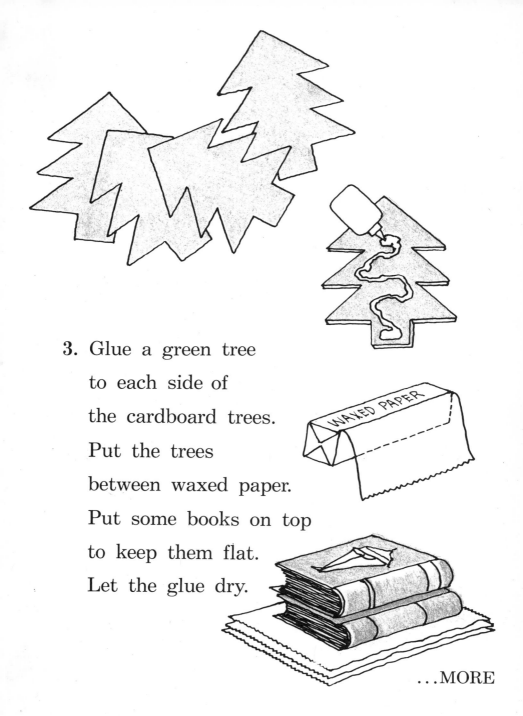

3. Glue a green tree
   to each side of
   the cardboard trees.
   Put the trees
   between waxed paper.
   Put some books on top
   to keep them flat.
   Let the glue dry.

...MORE

4. Make a cut in one tree at the top
and in the other at the bottom.

5. Fit them together.
Glue them in place.

6. Trim with stars,
glitter, or as you like.

String or Yarn Trims

1. Soak some string or yarn
   in liquid starch.

2. Shape the wet string
   or yarn as shown.
   Or make up your own shapes.
   Be sure the different parts
   of a design touch each other.
   Let them dry.

3. Tie a string to each shape
   to make a loop.

String and Plastic Trims

1. Soak some string
   in liquid starch.
   Make shapes on
   plastic wrap with it.

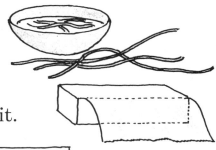

2. Put glue all around the shapes.
   Lay another piece
   of plastic wrap on top.
   Let the glue dry.

3. Cut out the shapes.

4. Punch a hole
through each shape.
Put a string through it.
Tie the string
to make a loop.

Stained Plastic

1. Mix black paint with
   a little liquid detergent.

2. Paint outlines
   on plastic wrap as shown.
   Or use your own ideas.

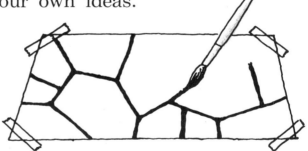

3. Mix food coloring
   with liquid detergent
   and a little glue.

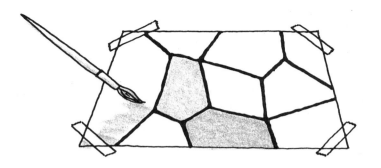

4. Fill in the outlines
   with paint.
   Let the paint dry.

5. Tape the plastic
   on a window
   with paper tape.

Santa Claus Face

1. Staple or glue
   a sheet of art paper
   to the top
   of a paper plate.

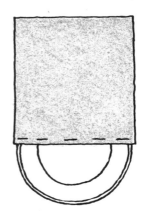

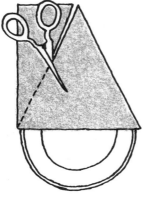

2. Cut as shown
   to make a Santa's hat.

3. Punch a hole
   in the top of the hat.
   Put a string
   through the hole.
   Tie it to make a loop.

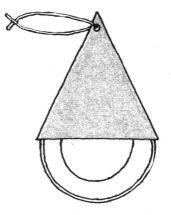

4. Glue cotton to the hat as shown.

5. Paint a Santa's face.

6. Glue on cotton for eyebrows. Glue cotton around the face to make a beard.

49

Star

1. Bend five paper straws in half.
   Place them on paper as shown.
   Glue them in place.
   Let the glue dry.

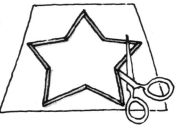

2. Cut around the star.
   This will be
   your pattern.

3. Use your pattern
   to draw a star
   on cardboard.
   Cut it out.
   Paint it or
   glue foil to it.

50

4. Glue the star
   to a small cardboard tube.
   The tube can be slipped
   over the top of a tree.

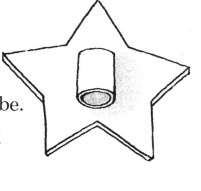

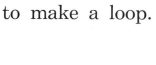

5. Use straws cut in half
   for a smaller star pattern.
   Do not glue
   the small star to a tube.
   Punch a hole in the star.
   Put a string through it.
   Tie the string
   to make a loop.

Star of David

1. Press three paper straws flat. Cut one straw in half.

2. Bend the two long straws as shown. Staple the short straws to them.

3. Staple in place to make a star.

4. Put a string through the top part of the star. Tie it to make a loop.

5. Or place the star
   on plastic wrap.
   Put glue all around it.
   Put plastic wrap on top.
   Let the glue dry.
   Cut around the star.

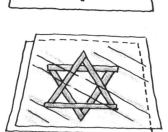

6. Punch a hole through the star.
   Put a string through it.
   Tie the string
   to make a loop.

Menorah

1. Cut a sheet
   of art paper in half.
   Make a roll
   from one half.
   Tape it in place.

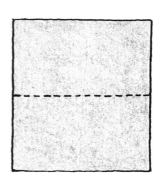

2. Punch nine small holes
   across the top of the roll.

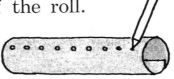

3. Cut the other piece
   of paper in half.
   Make a roll
   from one half.
   Tape it in place.

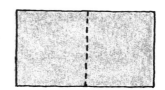

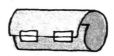

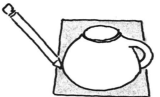

4. Cut a circle
   the size of a cup
   from the other piece.
   Cut another circle
   the same size
   from cardboard.
   Glue the two circles together.

5. Glue the shorter roll
   to the circle.
   Then glue a strip of paper
   across the top of the roll.

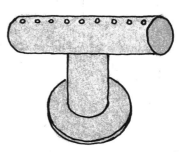

6. Glue the unpunched side
   of the longer roll
   to the shorter roll.
   Let the glue dry.

... MORE

7. Cut five straws in half.
   Glue small pieces
   of yellow paper
   to nine pieces of straw.

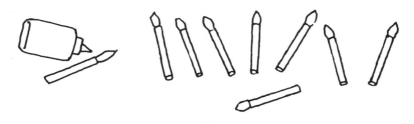

8. Put a straw candle
   in each hole.
   Put glue around
   each candle.
   Let the glue dry.

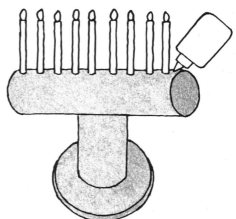

Straw Ball

1. Cut a lot of paper straws into halves or fourths. Cut one end of each into strips.

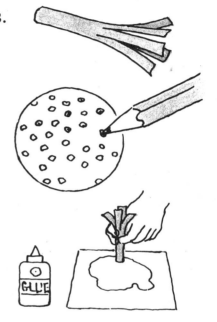

2. Punch holes all over a styrofoam ball. Dip the uncut straw ends in glue. Put a straw in each hole.

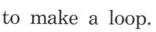

3. Bend a paper clip as shown. Hook it through the ball. Tie a string to it to make a loop.

Angel

1. Use a dinner plate
   for a pattern.
   Draw two circles
   on crepe paper.
   Cut them out.

2. Put the circles together.
   Fold them in half.
   Then fold them
   in half again.
   Cut as shown.

FOLD

FOLD

FOLD

3. Put glue around one end
   of a short cardboard tube.
   Fit one circle around it.
   Glue the other circle
   on top of the first.

4. Paint a face and hair
   on a styrofoam ball.
   Let the paint dry.
   Glue the ball
   to the top of the tube.

5. Bend a pipe cleaner
   as shown for a halo.
   Stick it into the head.

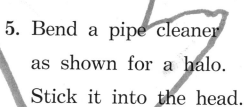

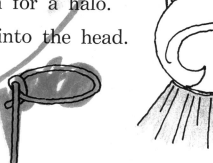

...MORE

59

6. Use wet starched yarn
(see page 43)
to make wings.
Shape them
on plastic wrap.
Shake glitter in them.

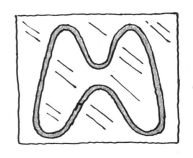

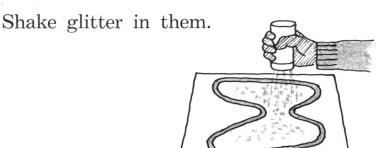

Put glue all around the yarn.
Lay another piece
of plastic wrap on top.
Let the glue dry.

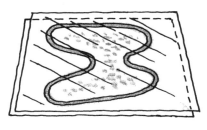

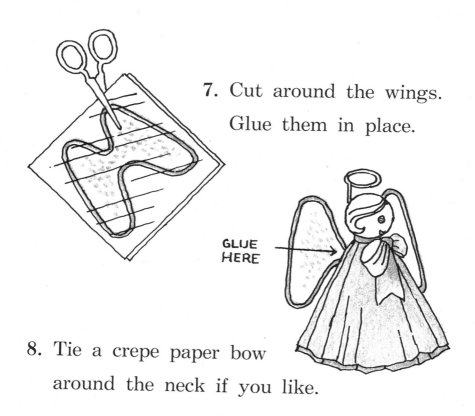

7. Cut around the wings.
Glue them in place.

GLUE
HERE

8. Tie a crepe paper bow
around the neck if you like.

61

Gift-Wrapping Paper

1. You can use any kind
   of paper for this.
   But tissue paper is best.

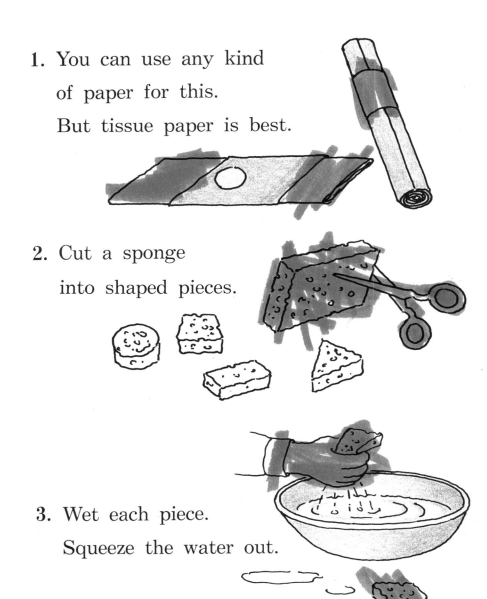

2. Cut a sponge
   into shaped pieces.

3. Wet each piece.
   Squeeze the water out.

4. Put paint
   into small bowls.
   Add a little water
   and mix well.

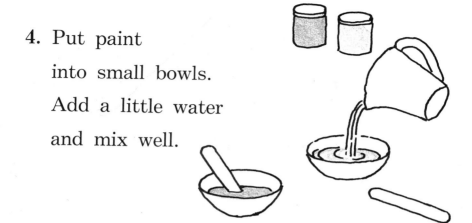

5. Dip a piece of sponge
   very lightly in the paint.
   Press it lightly on the paper.
   Let the paint dry.

Candy Candleholder

1. Make a slit in one side
   of a large gumdrop.
   Press a Life Saver candy
   in the slit.

2. Make a small hole
   in the top of the gumdrop.
   Put a birthday candle
   in the hole.

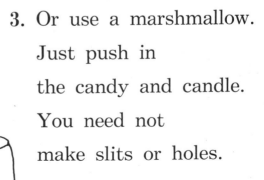

3. Or use a marshmallow.
   Just push in
   the candy and candle.
   You need not
   make slits or holes.